THE SUPERKIDS READING PROGRAM

SECOND GRADE

The
Superkids
Hit Second Grade

BY
PLEASANT T. ROWLAND

STORIES WRITTEN BY
VALERIE TRIPP

ILLUSTRATED BY
NORM BENDELL

DEVELOPED BY
ROWLAND READING FOUNDATION

ISBN 978-1-61436-579-2

1-888-378-9258
www.superkidsreading.com

Printed in the United States of America

3 4 5 6 7 8 9 10   997   21 20 19 18

The SUPERKIDS Hit Second Grade!

Cass

Oswald

Golly

Alf

Doc

Sal

Lily

Ms. Blossom

Icky

Tic

Tac

Toc

Frits

Ettabetta

Hot Rod

Contents

Unit 1

Chapter 1

Chapter 2

Unit 2

Chapter 3

Chapter 4

Unit 3

Chapter 5

Chapter 6

Unit 4

Chapter 7

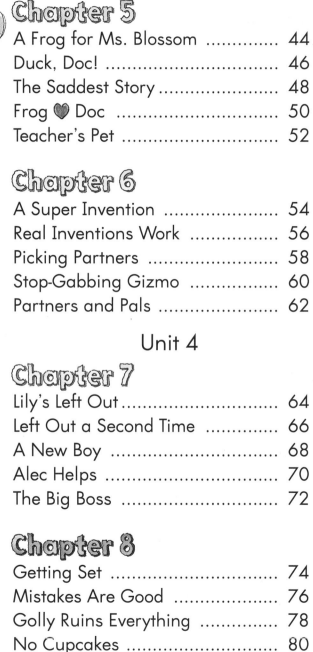

Chapter 8

Unit 5

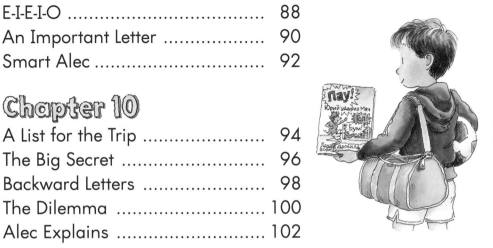

Chapter 9

Chapter 10

Unit 6

Chapter 11

Chapter 12

Unit 7

Chapter 13

Chapter 14

Unit 8

Chapter 15

Chapter 16

Chapter 1

The Best on the Planet

Alf's backpack went bump, bump, bump as he ran.

He spotted his pal Frits and ran up to him.

"Let's run to second grade," said Alf.

"OK!" said Frits. "Last kid to class is a rotten egg."

Alf and Frits ran fast,

past a bunch of kids,

past a big trash can,

and up the steps.

Zip! Zip! Zip!

At last, they got to class and skidded to a stop.

"I win," panted Alf. "I am the fastest kid on the planet!"

"OK," said Frits. "But I am the second fastest kid on the planet."

"And I am Ms. Blossom," said Ms. Blossom. "And my class is the best second grade on the planet!"

Sandwich Switch

"Yuck!" said Tic. "My dad put a ham sandwich in my lunch."

"Let's switch," said Tac. "My lunch is an egg-salad sandwich."

"Forget it!" said Tic. "I can't stand egg salad."

"I like it," said Toc. "Tic, if you like chicken, I can fix our problems. I have a chicken sandwich."

"OK," said Tic and Tac.

Toc put her chicken sandwich in Tic's lunch bag. She put Tic's ham sandwich in Tac's bag, and Tac's egg-salad sandwich in her bag.

The smell of the lunches was fantastic to Golly!
He ran up to Tic, Tac, and Toc.

"No, Golly," said Tac. "Get back on the bus."

But Golly did not get back on the bus. He hid in
the bushes until Tic, Tac, and Toc left. Then he trotted
fast to catch up to them—and their lunches!

Golly Grabs Lunch

Cass had a big cast on her leg. Clump-a-clump, clump-a-clunk went her crutches.

"Can we help you?" Tic said.

"Yes, thanks!" said Cass. She handed her lunch bag to Tic, but Golly ran up and—SNATCH! He got the lunch bag and sped off!

"Stop!" said Tic, Tac, and Toc. "Stop, stop, STOP!"

"Catch him!" said Cass. "I can't run!"

"We'll get him!" said Toc.

Lily Gets a Kiss

Tic, Tac, and Toc ran fast, but not as fast as Golly! On and on Golly ran until—CRASH! He ran smack into Lily. Golly let Cass's lunch drop. He began to jump up on Lily and lick her.

Tic, Tac, and Toc ran up. "Thanks, Lily," they said.

"Thanks?" said Lily.

"Yes, thanks a lot!" said Tac. "You got Cass's lunch back!"

"And I got a big, wet kiss from Golly," said Lily. "Yuck!"

Lily's Bad Luck

Lily got to second grade, but she was a big mess.
"I had such bad luck," she said to Ms. Blossom.

"I had to rush to catch the bus,
And mud got on my dress.
A big kid sat upon my lunch.
My sandwich is a mess.

"My backpack fell off of the bench.
It landed with a crash.
I went to scratch a bad, bad itch,
And, yuck, it was a rash.

"I had a dog jump up on me.
I did not like his kisses.
His lick was wet and, gosh, he stank
As much as rotten fishes!"

"Well, you had lots of
bad luck, Lily," said Ms.
Blossom. "I am glad you got
to second grade at last."

Chapter 2

Meet Ms. Blossom

When Sal got to class, he said, "Where is my desk? Who will I sit next to?"

Oswald said, "Sit next to me."

"OK," said Sal.

Oswald pretended to dust off a desk for Sal. "Best desk in the class," he said. "Just for you!"

"Thanks!" said Sal.

As Sal sat, Oswald said, "Ms. Blossom's class is full of fun stuff."

"But a lot of it is odd," said Sal. "Did you spot the blossoms on her desk and on her buttons and on her glasses? What's with that?"

"Well," said Oswald, "she _is_ Ms. Blossom. Get it? That's why she likes blossoms on her stuff."

15

Ms. Blossom's Flag

"OK, class," said Ms. Blossom. "Let's stand up and stretch."

"That's a bit odd," said Doc to Cass.

"Pretend you are a plant," said Ms. Blossom. "You have a stem. It is your back. Stretch it up and lift your fists.

"Next, pretend your fist is the bud. Then, POP! The bud pops into a big blossom."

Pop, pop, pop went the Superkids' hands. "Pop! Pop! Pop!" the Superkids said.

"That is splendid," said Ms. Blossom. "Just splendid. You will stretch yourself here in second grade, just as you can stretch your back and hands. And when you do the best you can, you will . . ."

But Ms. Blossom did not finish. She just held up a flag. The flag said,

Blossom in Second Grade

17

The Wishes Game

"Do you like wishes?" said Ms. Blossom.

"Yes!" said the Superkids.

"Then let's play the Wishes Game," said Ms. Blossom. "I'll ask you what you wish for. You'll think, and then you'll write your wishes."

"OK!" said the Superkids.

Ms. Blossom said, "What do you wish we had in our class?"

The Superkids had to stop and think. Then they began to write their wishes. Ms. Blossom went from desk to desk to help them spell.

Tac said, "Do you like my wish, Ms. Blossom?"

Tac

I wish we had a big, big frog for our class pet.

"Yes, I do!" said Ms. Blossom. "I like frogs! Why not add a big, big bug for the frog to have for lunch?"

"That's fun," said Tac, and she added a big bug to her sketch.

The Superkids' Wishes

Next, Ms. Blossom said, "What do you wish you could read about in second grade?"

In a flash, the Superkids handed their wishes to Ms. Blossom. Here they are:

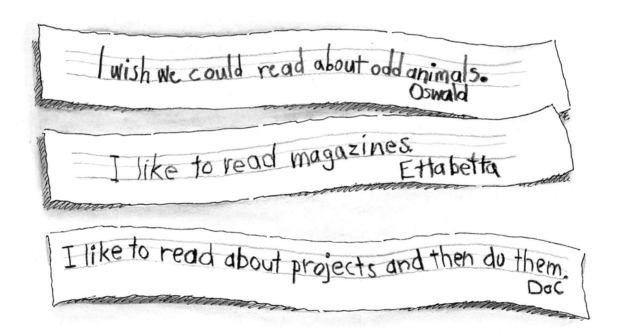

I wish we could read about odd animals.
Oswald

I like to read magazines.
Ettabetta

I like to read about projects and then do them.
Doc

I wish we could read about kids like us.
Cass

I like to read things just for fun.
Lily

Ms. Blossom began to read the Superkids' wishes.

"Well," she said. "You can have what you wish for! Here is what you get to read. It's a magazine for kids in second grade just like you."

And it's SUPER!

SUPER!

Ms. Blossom handed the Superkids their magazines. The kids began to grin. SUPER was super!

23

Chapter 3

Ms. Blossom's Gift

"B-r-i-n-g-g!" the bell rang. Ms. Blossom began to pass some bags to the Superkids. "I have a gift for you," she said.

Quick as a wink, the kids stuck their hands into the bags to get their presents. But the presents were just dull little lumps, like rocks.

"Look at this thing," said Toc. "What an odd present."

"It smells like a mud puddle," said Tac. "Yuck!"

Ms. Blossom said, "Can any of you tell me what the gift is?"

Alf's hand shot up. "I can!" he said.

Ms. Blossom was just about to pick Alf, but Ettabetta began to yell,

It's a bulb! It's a bulb!

"You forgot to put your hand up, Ettabetta," said Ms. Blossom. "But, yes, the gift is a daffodil bulb. We will plant our bulbs and when spring comes, daffodils will pop up and we will have lots of blossoms."

The kids began to clap. They all had big grins. All but Alf, that is.

Bugging

"This is a very good time to plant your new bulbs," said Ms. Blossom. "Come with me!"

As the Superkids left the class, Alf began to bug Ettabetta. He pretended that his hand was a bumblebee.

"Buzz, buzz, buzz," he said. He began to tickle Ettabetta. "This bee can sting you."

And with a little pinch, Alf's bee stung Ettabetta's neck.

"Stop it," said Ettabetta.

She batted at Alf's hand. But Alf kept buzzing at Ettabetta and pinching her neck.

"Quit it, Alf," she said. "Just stop bugging me."

But Alf did not stop acting like a pest.

Ettabetta got mad. She kept batting at his hand until at last—WHACK! She hit him on the chin. And THUD! He fell on his bottom with a THUMP!

The class got very, very still.

"Gosh," said Doc with a gasp. "What will Ms. Blossom do?"

Too Strict?

"This is not how we act in second grade," Ms. Blossom said to Alf and Ettabetta. "You must sit back at your desks. Sit there until I come to get you."

"Yes, Ms. Blossom," said Alf and Ettabetta. They plodded to their desks and sat.

Ms. Blossom led the rest of the class up some steps that went to the roof.

"This is a good spot to plant bulbs," said Ms. Blossom. "They must have lots of sun. And dogs can't get up to the roof and dig them up. Plant your bulbs in these long boxes."

As Cass and Doc were planting,
Cass said, "Do you think Ms. Blossom
was too strict with Alf and Ettabetta?"

"No," said Doc. "They were acting up.
Ms. Blossom had to punish them.
She is strict, but I like her."

"I do too," said Cass.

29

A Second Beginning

Ms. Blossom went back to Alf and Ettabetta. They were still sitting at their desks looking very sad.

"Ettabetta," said Ms. Blossom, "tell me why you hit Alf."

"He was pinching me, and I got mad," said Ettabetta.

"I didn't mean to make Ettabetta mad," said Alf. "I was just bugging her for a little fun."

"Bugging can switch from fun to mean very fast," said Ms. Blossom.

Alf put his chin on his hand. He felt sad. "I wish second grade had just begun," he said.

"Me too," said Ettabetta. "I wish I hadn't hit you, Alf."

"OK, Alf and Ettabetta," said Ms. Blossom. "Second grade can have a second beginning for you. Let's pretend it has just begun. Alf, will you help Ettabetta plant her bulb?"

"I will be glad to," said Alf.

"And Ettabetta, will you help Alf?" said Ms. Blossom.

"Yes," said Ettabetta with a grin.

"Splendid," said Ms. Blossom. "Just splendid. Come with me and bring your bulbs."

Why Alf Did It

"Plant your bulbs in the long boxes," Ms. Blossom said to Alf and Ettabetta. "Then you can have lunch." She went to inspect the bulbs the rest of the class had planted.

As the two kids planted their bulbs, Ettabetta said, "Alf, why did you pick me to bug?"

"Well," said Alf, "I was a little mad at you."

"Why?" said Ettabetta. "What did I do?"

"When Ms. Blossom was asking what her gift was," said Alf, "I put my hand up. I wanted to tell her. But you began to yell, 'It's a bulb! It's a bulb!'"

"I didn't stop to think," said Ettabetta. "I won't do that again."

"Good," said Alf. "Then I won't bug you again."

"Very good!" said Ettabetta. "In fact, that will be just splendid!"

Chapter 4

The Soap Song

Ms. Blossom said, "Class, each day before lunch, you must clean your hands at the sink."

"What if we forget?" said Cass.

"That's a problem," said Ms. Blossom. "Who can think of how to help?"

"We can put up a note like this," said Tic.

"Ms. Blossom, you could get a bottle of soap bubbles," said Doc with a giggle. "When it's time for lunch, you could blow bubbles at us."

"I have an idea," said Icky. "Before lunch, we can sing a song like this." Icky began to sing:

"Scrub, scrub, scrub your hands,
Just before you eat.
Soap 'em, rinse 'em, dry 'em off.
Keep 'em clean and neat."

"And that <u>song</u> is neat!" said Ms. Blossom. "We'll sing it each day!"

Icky's Yucky Lunch

Icky ate the same lunch each day. It was a peanut butter sandwich with the crusts cut off, a green apple, a little box of raisins, milk, and carrot sticks. Sometimes, Icky's mom printed on his napkin, "Have a good day!"

Many times Icky's mom said, "Wouldn't you like something new, Icky?" But he said, "No thanks! I like my lunch <u>just</u> like it is." And he did!

Then one day, Icky's dad made his lunch. What a mistake <u>that</u> was!

His dad didn't cut the crusts off the peanut butter sandwich. He put jam on it, so it was pink and stuck to Icky's hands. He gave Icky a red apple, a banana, and grapes, but no milk, raisins, or carrots. The napkin was a leftover that had "Happy New Year!" on it.

"This lunch is a mess!" Icky said. He was just about to toss his yucky lunch into the trash can when he felt a hand on his back. "Just a second!" someone said. It was Ms. Blossom.

37

A Little Bit, A Little Bite

"Icky, I cannot let you toss your lunch into the trash," Ms. Blossom said.

"But Ms. Blossom," said Icky. "I don't like it."

"Well, how can you tell if you didn't try it?" said Ms. Blossom. "Come sit next to me. I have an idea. You cut up this sandwich into little squares while I cut up the apple, banana, and grapes."

Ms. Blossom made the fruit into fruit salad. Then she got Icky a carton of milk and handed him a plastic fork. "Try your lunch now," she said.

It felt funny to eat a sandwich with a fork, but at least Icky's hands didn't get sticky.

After just three bites, Icky had to admit that the sandwich was not bad. The milk was quite good, and the fruit salad was fantastic.

Before long, Icky had eaten his whole lunch!

"Thank you, Ms. Blossom," he said. "That lunch was really pretty good."

"It's best to try new things a little bit at a time," said Ms. Blossom.

"Or a little <u>bite</u> at a time!" said Icky with a smile.

Panic

Ms. Blossom handed a quiz to each Superkid. "This is the first test you will do in second grade," she said. "Try your best."

Frits put his name on the top of his quiz. He tried to read the first line, but he could not. He tried to read the second line, but it was just as difficult.

Frits felt his cheeks get hot. "I can't do this test," he said to himself. "Why is it just a mess of lines to me?"

He began to panic and wanted to cry. "It is only the beginning of second grade, and I can't do the first test."

Frits tried and tried many times. Then he gave up and simply put scribbles on the lines. He handed in his test just to get rid of it.

Second Fastest

When it was time to go home, Frits put on his backpack.

Ms. Blossom was at her desk. "Wait, Frits," she said. She had his test in her hand. "You did not finish your test. Why?"

Frits could barely speak. "Oh, Ms. Blossom," he said softly. "The test was so difficult for me. I began to panic, and I just forgot how to read."

"Many children panic when they take a test," said Ms. Blossom, "and things seem to fly out of their brains. But they get better at tests as the year goes on."

"Can I still be in second grade?" said Frits.

"Yes, indeed!" said Ms. Blossom. "We need you in our class." She gave Frits a wink. "I think you will get better at tests fast. You <u>are</u> the fastest kid on the planet, aren't you?"

"No," said Frits with a grin. "I am only the second fastest, but I will try my best."

"Splendid," said Ms. Blossom. "Just splendid."

Chapter 5

A Frog for Ms. Blossom

On a very rainy day, Tac and Doc were skipping along to school when Tac came to a sudden stop. "Shh!" she said.

"What is it?" said Doc.

"I think I hear a frog," said Tac. "Stay still."

"Ribbit, ribbit," went the frog.

Ribbit, ribbit.

"It <u>is</u> a frog," said Tac, "and it's in this bush. Let's catch it!"

"You've got to be kidding!" said Doc. "Why?"

"I like frogs," said Tac. "And I think Ms. Blossom would like a frog for our class pet."

"Frogs and toads are yucky," said Doc.

"Not to Ms. Blossom and me," said Tac. She bent over. "There it is!" she said. She dove into the bush to grab the frog.

But as Tac dove <u>in</u>, the frog shot <u>out</u>—straight at Doc!

45

Duck, Doc!

SMACK! The frog hit Doc in the nose. "EEK!" Doc began to screech.

"Catch it!" said Tac, jumping out of the bush.

But Doc flung her umbrella into the air and ran off. The umbrella landed in a puddle, and the frog landed in the umbrella.

Ribbit?

Tac crept next to the umbrella. She was just reaching out to grab the frog when Doc came back. "Stay away," Tac said to Doc.

But Tac was too late. The frog shot out of the umbrella and straight at Doc for the second time!

"Duck, Doc!" said Tac.

"Help!" said Doc. She fell back and landed in the puddle. SPLASH! went Doc. SPLASH! went the frog.

The Saddest Story

By now, the frog was as upset as Doc was. Off it went, hip, hop, hip, hop, as fast as it could and hid in the bush.

"Gosh, Tac," said Doc. "I'm sorry. Because of me, you lost your frog."

"That's OK," said Tac. "I'm sorry you got wet and muddy because of me."

"Well, it was really because of the frog," Doc said with a grin. She and Tac began to giggle.

"Come on," said Tac at last. "We'll be late." Tac and Doc ran the rest of the way to school.

When they got there, Ms. Blossom said, "Today we are going to have Show-and-Tell. I hope you will tell us how you got so wet."

"It's a sad story," said Tac, "about a frog."

"The saddest story ever <u>toad</u>," said Doc.

Frog ♥ Doc

The next day as Doc was going to school, what should jump out in front of her? The frog!

"Not you again," said Doc. "Go away!"

The frog just sat there.

"Get lost!" said Doc.

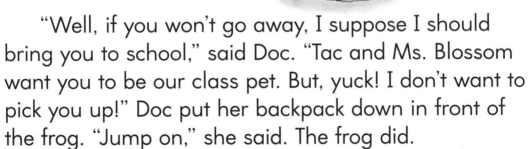

"Ribbit," went the frog.

"Well, if you won't go away, I suppose I should bring you to school," said Doc. "Tac and Ms. Blossom want you to be our class pet. But, yuck! I don't want to pick you up!" Doc put her backpack down in front of the frog. "Jump on," she said. The frog did.

"Now stay put," Doc said. The frog did. Doc held her backpack way out in front of her and trotted along to school.

When she got there, she put her backpack on Tac's desk. "Here," she said.

"Our frog! How did you catch it?" said Tac in amazement.

"Catch it?" said Doc. "I can't get rid of it! This frog loves me!"

"Ribbit!" went the frog.

Teacher's Pet

"Look, Ms. Blossom," said Tac. "Here's the frog that Doc and I lost before."

"My goodness!" said Ms. Blossom.

"It's for you," said Doc. "Tac said you wanted a frog for a pet."

"Well," said Ms. Blossom. "I <u>do</u> like frogs. And this frog is very handsome. But I think it is a bit big. It would be sad in our tank because it would not have room to hop."

"It would be unhappy because it would be <u>unhoppy</u>," joked Doc.

"Yes, I'm afraid so," said Ms. Blossom with a smile.

Tac was very sad.

"Here is what we'll do," said Ms. Blossom. "The frog can visit us today. Then you can set it free on your way home from school."

"OK," said Tac.

Ms. Blossom gave Tac a hug. "Thank you," she said. "Just for today, the frog will be the teacher's pet!"

Chapter 6

A Super Invention

Ms. Blossom held up SUPER and said, "Look at the funny inventions. Can you tell us what an invention is, Ettabetta?"

Ettabetta didn't say anything. She was busy reading SUPER and didn't hear Ms. Blossom.

Tic gave Ettabetta a quick poke, and Ettabetta sat up.

Ms. Blossom said, "SUPER is full of fun things to read, Ettabetta. But you must stay with the class. I asked you what an invention is."

"An invention is something new that people think up," said Ettabetta. "Inventions can make things easy and more fun to do."

"Splendid," said Ms. Blossom. "Who can tell us an example of an invention?"

"I can!" said Icky. "SUPER is a super invention. It makes second grade better and much more fun."

Inventions
1. Make things easy to do.
2. Make things better.
3. Make things fun.
4. Make it possible to do new things.

Real Inventions Work

"Class," said Ms. Blossom, "would you like to invent things like the kids in SUPER did?"

"Yes!" the kids yelled.

"What if we can't think of an invention?" asked Doc.

"Inventing is like the Wishes Game," said Ms. Blossom. "Inventors think of something they wish they had. Maybe it's something to fix a problem, or a new way to do things. Next, inventors think of how to make what they're wishing for. And then they try to do it."

"I'm going to invent the fastest bike!" said Hot Rod.

"I'm going to invent a robot that plays soccer," said Oswald.

"I'll invent rockets that help me fly," said Tic.

"Not so fast!" said Ms. Blossom. "Your inventions must be real. Real inventions really work. That's how they are different from wishes or dreams."

Picking Partners

"Let's begin work on your inventions," said Ms. Blossom. "It's time to pick partners."

Quickly, Cass said, "Ettabetta, be my partner!"

"But Ettabetta," said Lily, "I wanted you to be <u>my</u> partner."

"Why don't the three of us work together?" asked Ettabetta.

"That would be good," said Lily.

"But partner means two," said Cass.

Lily felt upset. Didn't Cass want to work with her? She felt a bit better when Ms. Blossom said the three girls could work together.

"I have lots of good ideas," said Cass.

"So do I," said Lily.

"Let's meet after school to discuss them," said Ettabetta.

"I can't today," said Lily. "I have Chinese lessons."

"Well," Cass said briskly, "then Ettabetta and I will meet, and we'll tell you about it after."

"OK," said Lily. But she didn't feel OK. She felt left out.

Stop-Gabbing Gizmo

Hot Rod asked Sal, "Want to be partners?"

"OK," said Sal.

"So," said Hot Rod, "what do you want to invent?"

"Well," said Sal, "I liked what you said about inventing a fast bike. Did you see those BMX bikes on TV?"

"Yes!" said Hot Rod. "They were really fast!"

"I bet a BMX bike costs a lot," said Sal.

"That kid Sam has a BMX bike," said Hot Rod.

"Does he go to our school?" asked Sal.

"No," said Hot Rod. But he stopped speaking when Ms. Blossom came by his desk. She looked a little cross.

"I hope you two are inventing a gizmo that will make you stop gabbing and get to work!" she said. "You need it!"

61

Partners and Pals

At lunch, Icky said, "What are you going to invent, Doc?"

"Well," said Doc. "I like making things, but I have never invented anything brand-new. Have you?"

"I have lots of plans for inventions in my desk," said Icky, "but they just stay there. I am not good at making things."

"You have plans, and I don't," said Doc grinning. "But I can make things, and you can't. Let's team up."

"OK!" said Icky.

After lunch, Icky came to Doc with his plans. He had so many that some began flying off!

"Yikes!" said Doc. "You <u>do</u> have a lot of plans."

"They're a mess," said Icky.

"Let's lay them all out," said Doc. "Then we can pick the best plan."

"Thanks, Doc," said Icky. "We'll be good partners!"

Chapter 7

Lily's Left Out

The next morning, Lily met up with Cass and Ettabetta before school.

"How was the meeting about our invention?" Lily asked. "Did you make a list of ideas?"

"The meeting was fun," said Cass. "Ettabetta's mom gave us cupcakes."

"And the cupcakes gave us a fantastic idea," said Ettabetta. "We are going to invent a cupcake froster."

"But I didn't tell you <u>my</u> idea yet," said Lily. "I was thinking we could invent an ice-skating board."

"But we like our idea better," said Ettabetta.

"Well, I don't," said Lily.

The girls did not say anything for a while.

Then Cass said, "Lily, maybe you should team up with Sal and Hot Rod. I bet they would like your idea."

"And I bet you would like the idea of me being on another team," said Lily in a huff. "You never did want me on yours!"

Left Out a Second Time

In art class, Ettabetta and Cass started whispering together about their cupcake froster.

It made Lily feel lonely, so she got up and went to speak to Hot Rod and Sal.

"Do you want to work with me on my invention?" Lily asked them. "It's an ice-skating board."

"That's a neat idea, Lily," said Hot Rod. "But Sal and I are going to invent something to make our bikes go faster."

"Do you want to team up with us?" asked Sal. "We could use the help."

"We're not such good partners," admitted Hot Rod. "We don't even have a sketch yet!"

"Well, thanks," said Lily. "But I really want to make my invention. So it looks like I'll have to work alone."

"OK, then," said Sal. "Good luck!"

A New Boy

The next morning, there was a new boy in the Superkids' class. Ms. Blossom said, "Boys and girls, this is Alec."

The Superkids said, "Hi, Alec!" The new boy just grinned. He didn't say anything.

"Alec," said Ms. Blossom. "The kids have picked partners, and they are making inventions."

Alec's grin got a little bigger.

"Now!" said Ms. Blossom. "Who needs a partner?"

Lily hesitated and then raised her hand just a little. She couldn't tell if the new kid would be a good partner or not.

"Splendid!" said Ms. Blossom. "Alec, sit next to Lily."

When Alec sat down, Lily put her sketch on his desk. "This is my invention," she said.

Alec looked at the plan very closely, which made Lily happy. Maybe at last she had a partner who liked her idea as much as she did!

Alec Helps

The odd thing about Alec was that he hardly ever spoke. The whole time Lily explained her ice-skating board to him, he didn't say a thing.

"Do you like it?" she asked. Alec nodded.

"Do you think it will work?" asked Lily. Alec shrugged.

"Is that a yes?" asked Lily. Alec grinned.

Lily felt a little angry. She began to think that she would have to do all the work by herself. If Alec never spoke, how could he be a good partner and help her?

But when Lily came back after lunch, she was surprised to see some sketches on her desk. They showed her ice-skating board, but sketched lots of different times to show the bottom, the top, and the sides. The sketches were really good.

"Did you do these?" Lily asked Alec.

Alec nodded, and this time Lily didn't feel a bit angry.

The Big Boss

The kids began to bring parts for their inventions from home.

Ettabetta said, "Cass, did you bring the tubes?"

"I forgot," said Cass. "What do we need them for?"

"We need tubes to squirt the frosting," said Ettabetta. "Look at the plan!" She held up a sketch of the cupcake froster.

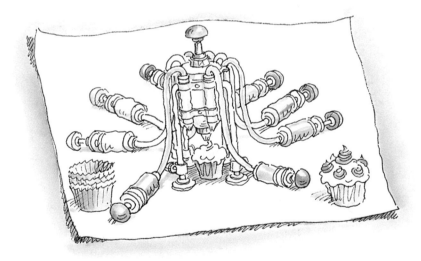

"Wait," said Cass. "The froster looks like a big spider. I don't remember these long tubes."

"I added those," said Ettabetta.

"Well, you should have asked me before you added stuff," said Cass. "You're not the big boss."

"And <u>you're</u> not a big help!" said Ettabetta.

Just then, Tic came past and looked at the sketch. "A cupcake froster!" she said. "What fun!"

Cass and Ettabetta looked at each other.

"We forgot that partners are supposed to be friends," said Cass.

"And that projects are supposed to be fun," said Ettabetta with a grin.

Chapter 8

Getting Set

Invention Day!

Ms. Blossom's second graders will display their inventions this Friday morning at nine o'clock. Come and see!!

Alf Lily Ettabetta Icky Hot Rod Sal Oswald Alec Cass Doc Tic Tac Toe Frits

Ms. Blossom's class invited the third graders to come see their inventions. All the kids had jobs to do before the big day.

"I'm painting this big banner," said Hot Rod to Lily. "What are you doing?"

"I'm going to bring sugar cookies," said Lily.

"Cookies?" said Hot Rod. "Will we need them? Won't we be eating decorated cupcakes? Doesn't Cass and Ettabetta's invention work?"

"Don't ask me," said Lily.

"Oh," said Hot Rod. "How is your invention?"

"Good," said Lily. "The new boy, Alec, was a big help. He can draw really well. He could help you with that banner. Just don't be surprised if he doesn't say anything. He doesn't like to talk."

"Then Alec would be the perfect kid for me to work with! Ms. Blossom said that Sal and I talk too much," said Hot Rod.

Mistakes Are Good

Ms. Blossom said, "Frits, would you like to welcome the third graders with a short speech?"

"Me?" asked Frits. He was surprised.

"Yes," said Ms. Blossom. "You have been working hard. Your reading and spelling are better every day, and you are doing much better on your tests."

Frits grinned. He would be so proud to stand up in front of all the children. But then he realized that he would be nervous too. He hesitated before answering, "Thanks, Ms. Blossom, but I can't do it. I still make lots of mistakes."

"We all make mistakes," said Ms. Blossom. "And thank goodness we do, because mistakes show us what we need to work on. I think you could do a fine job."

"Well, OK. I'll try," said Frits.

"Splendid!" said Ms. Blossom.

Golly Ruins Everything

At last the big day came! Cass and Ettabetta set off for school early with their cupcakes and frosting.

"I think <u>all</u> the kids will like our invention the best," said Ettabetta happily.

Just as the girls were going past the Superkids' bus, it started to rain hard.

"Help!" said Cass. "The cupcakes will be ruined if they get wet."

"Wait here," said Ettabetta. "There's an umbrella on the bus. I'll get it."

"Hurry!" said Cass.

Ettabetta was back in a flash with the umbrella. Golly, who had been sleeping on the bus, trotted along after her.

When Golly saw the cupcakes, he galloped past Ettabetta and jumped up onto Cass. The cupcakes went flying. They rained down on Cass and Ettabetta, tumbling onto the pavement and plopping into mud puddles. Golly gobbled them up, mud and all.

No Cupcakes

By the time Cass and Ettabetta got to class, all the other kids were busy setting up their inventions.

"Well," said Cass sadly. "Let's make the best of it. Let's attach the tubes to the froster. Maybe the kids will understand how our invention is supposed to work even without the cupcakes."

Hot Rod looked at the empty plate. "Where are the cupcakes?" he asked. "What happened?"

"Golly ate them," said Cass.

"That's the worst thing ever!" said Sal. "What will you do?"

"There's not much we <u>can</u> do," said Ettabetta.

Just then the third graders began to arrive, and the Superkids had to take their seats. Cass and Ettabetta went back to their desks and plopped down.

"I wish we could invent a machine to make us invisible," said Cass.

"Me too," said Ettabetta sadly.

81

Frosting

"Welcome, third graders!" said Frits proudly. "We hope you will ask us about our inventions. We had fun making them! Thank you for coming."

All the kids clapped. Then the second graders rushed to stand next to their inventions. Cass and Ettabetta did not rush. What good was their invention if they couldn't show how it was supposed to work?

As they got close to the froster, a third-grade girl said to them, "This is neat! Can you show us how it works?"

"Can we eat one after it's decorated?" asked a boy.

Cass and Ettabetta were confused. There were no cupcakes to eat. Then they looked down at the plate. Someone had put cookies on it so that they could demonstrate their invention. What a wonderful surprise!

"Where did these cookies come from?" Ettabetta asked Cass. They looked up and saw Lily smiling at them.

"Lily, you did it! Come and help us frost the cookies," said Cass.

"We're partners after all," said Ettabetta. "Partners and pals. Isn't that the frosting on the cake?"

Chapter 9

Mystery Kid

Alec was a mystery kid. He seemed to understand what the Superkids said, but he never talked.

Sal wondered if Alec spoke Spanish. *"¿Hablas español?"* Sal asked. That means, "Do you speak Spanish?" Alec said nothing.

Tic spoke French. She said, *"Parles-tu français?"* That means, "Do you speak French?" Alec still said nothing.

Lily was learning Chinese, so she said, *"Ni hui shuo zhong wen ma?"* That means, "Do you speak Chinese?" Alec looked confused.

"Well," said Sal with a shrug, "it doesn't really matter. Want to play soccer?"

Alec grinned. He flipped the ball from his toe to his hands, twirled it on one finger, tossed it up into the air, and kicked it—all the way into the goal.

What a surprise! Sal, Tic, and Lily just looked at each other. Now <u>they</u> were the ones who were speechless!

Soccer Star

The soccer game was close. The Superkids were winning by only one point. Then a kid on the other team kicked the ball hard. WHAM! The ball shot past all the Superkids and nearly went into the goal.

But at the last second, Alec dove for the ball and stopped it! The Superkids won.

Sal ran up to Alec and thumped him on the back. "Good game, Alec," he said. Alec looked very happy, but he said nothing. He just tossed the ball to Sal, waved, and left for home.

"Alec is a really good goalie," said Tic. "He doesn't say much, but he thinks fast."

"When it comes to soccer, I'd rather have a smart player than a smart talker," said Sal. "I wonder how he learned to play ball like that."

"Well," said Lily, "that's <u>another</u> mystery about Alec."

E-I-E-I-O

The next day, Ms. Blossom's class checked on all the bulbs they had planted. Tic helped Alec plant his bulb.

"Alec's bulb will blossom a little later than the rest," said Ms. Blossom. "But that's fine. Plants blossom at different times. We'll pick <u>our</u> blossoms in the spring. But some plants, like apples and pumpkins, are being picked on farms now."

88

Ms. Blossom smiled. "Would you like to visit a farm?" she asked.

"Yes!" said the class. Everyone cheered and started to make animal noises.

Ms. Blossom started to act silly too. She sang: "We are going to a farm . . ."

And the Superkids called out, "E-I-E-I-O!"

89

An Important Letter

Ms. Blossom handed out letters about the class trip. "Take your letter home," she said. "Ask an adult to read it and sign it. Then bring it back to me. You can't go on our Fall on the Farm trip if you don't turn in a signed letter."

The next morning, Sal met Oswald and Alec at the bus stop. It was such a rainy day!

"Got your signed letter?" Oswald asked.

"Yup!" said Sal. He took the letter out of his backpack, waved it like a flag, and then quickly slipped it into his raincoat pocket so it wouldn't get wet.

"Do you have your signed letter, Alec?" Oswald asked.

Alec hesitated, then nodded yes.

"Good!" said Oswald. "That letter is important, and Ms. Blossom is strict about important stuff. Isn't she, Sal?"

"Absolutely!" said Sal.

Smart Alec

Before class, Ms. Blossom asked, "Does anyone have a letter to turn in?"

Sal reached into his backpack. "That's odd," he said. "I just saw it!" He looked into his backpack, then turned it upside down on his desk. Everything spilled out. Sal looked and looked, but his letter about the class trip was not there. He was flustered. "Ms. Blossom, my mom <u>did</u> sign the letter," he said. "And I put it in my backpack. But now it's lost."

"I'll print a new letter for you today," said Ms. Blossom. "But be more careful this time."

Just then, Alec jumped up from his desk. He ran to Sal's cubby, put his hand in the pocket of Sal's raincoat—and pulled out the letter!

Chapter 10

A List for the Trip

"Let's make a list for our class trip," said Ms. Blossom. She used a marker to write on the flip chart.

Fall on the Farm

Things We Need

"We need to bring lunches," said Oswald.

Ms. Blossom put Lunches on the list.

Toc said, "We need jackets in case it gets chilly."

Ms. Blossom put Jackets on the list.

Alf said, "We all need to bring extra sneakers and socks in case our feet get wet."

"Toc and Alf, you are too fussy!" said Tac.

"Yes," agreed Oswald. "That extra stuff is not important."

"I'll tell you what <u>is</u> important," said Ms. Blossom. "Some of you have not turned in your letters yet. Tomorrow is the last day to do so. Remember, you <u>must</u> hand in your letter signed by a grownup, or you will not be allowed to go on the trip."

The Big Secret

"I can't wait to go to the farm!" said Doc at lunch. "Ms. Blossom said we'll get to milk cows."

"I think the hayride will be the best part of the trip," said Sal. "Don't you, Icky?"

Icky shrugged.

"You don't seem very happy about our trip," said Doc. "What's the matter?"

"Nothing," said Icky.

"Then why are you being such a grouch?" Sal asked. "What's bothering you?"

Icky frowned. "I can't say anything here," he said. "Meet me on the playground after lunch."

"Gosh!" said Frits. "What's your big secret?"

"It isn't really <u>my</u> secret," said Icky. "That's the problem! Just meet me outside later, and I'll explain."

Backward Letters

After lunch, the Superkids met by the soccer goal.

"So what's the secret?" asked Sal.

Icky said, "Didn't Ms. Blossom say you couldn't go on the class trip without a letter signed by a grownup?"

"Yes," said Frits.

"Well," said Icky, "when I turned in my letter today, I saw Alec's. It was on top of the pile. I think Alec only <u>pretended</u> a grownup signed it. I think he really signed it himself."

"But that would be lying," said Doc. "Alec's a good kid! He wouldn't lie. What makes you think that Alec signed his own letter?"

"Because some of the letters in the name were backward," said Icky.

"What do you mean?" asked Frits.

"I'll show you," said Icky. He printed letters in the dirt with his finger. "Grownups don't write this way."

The Dilemma

"Should I tell Ms. Blossom what I think Alec did?" Icky asked.

"No," said Doc. "Maybe Alec didn't understand how important the signed letter was."

"I think he did," said Sal. "Oswald and I spoke to him about it, and he seemed to understand."

"But if we tell Ms. Blossom that Alec lied, she won't let him go on the trip," said Icky.

"I had a problem at the beginning of second grade," said Frits. "I sort of forgot how to read. I didn't want to tell anyone, so I kept it secret. But I admitted it to Ms. Blossom, and she was really terrific about it. I think we should tell her about Alec. She'll help him the way she helped me."

"But shouldn't we ask Alec about it first, before we tell on him?" said Sal. "Maybe he can explain."

"Who will ask him?" said Doc. "He could get mad."

"I'll do it," said Sal.

101

Alec Explains

As Sal and Alec walked to soccer, Sal said, "Alec, who signed your letter about the class trip?"

"*Babushka*," said Alec. "Grandmother."

"But some of the letters were backward," said Sal.

"Russian," said Alec.

"Oh, she was <u>rushing</u>," said Sal. "Your grandmother wrote backward because she was <u>rushing</u>!"

"No!" said Alec. "<u>Russian</u>. From Russia. Letters look different. See?" Alec pulled a comic out of his backpack. Sal saw that some letters were the same as in English, but some letters looked backward.

"Oh!" said Sal. "You speak Russian. Why didn't you say so a long time ago?"

"My English is bad," said Alec. "It's better I'm quiet."

"No, it's better if you speak up and talk more," said Sal. "When I came here, I spoke only Spanish. But the more English I spoke, the better I got."

"OK," Alec grinned. "Soon, my English gets good."

"Just like your soccer," said Sal.

Chapter 11

Big Backpacks

At last the day came for the class trip to the farm. All the kids had backpacks with food for lunch. Alf's backpack was big because he had stuffed extra sneakers and socks in it. Toc's backpack was big because she had stuffed in a warm jacket and some boots. There was no room under the seat for the big bags. So they held their bags on their laps.

Tac and Oswald were sitting in front of Toc and Alf. Tac began to tease. "Oh, Oswald," said Tac. She spoke loudly so that Alf and Toc could hear. "I forgot my raincoat, boots, and umbrella! What will I do if it <u>rains</u> while we're at the farm?"

"Oh, Tac, I forgot my snow pants, winter coat, mittens, and scarf," said Oswald. "What will I do if it <u>snows</u> while we're at the farm?"

"Quit teasing," said Alf. "<u>We're</u> prepared for this trip and <u>you're</u> not. You'll be sorry."

Baby

When the Superkids got off the bus, they met the farmer, Ms. Gibson. "Welcome to Fall on the Farm!" she said. "We'll look around the barn first."

The barn was dark and cool inside. It smelled of hay. The kids went up the ladder into the hayloft and tossed hay down to the horses in their stalls.

Then Ms. Gibson showed them how to milk a cow. Everyone took a turn sitting on the wooden stool and squirting milk into the bucket.

"I may never drink milk again," Cass whispered to Tic.

Outside, the barnyard was busy and noisy. Chickens clucked, ducks quacked, and pigs oinked.

A big, fat goose honked. "Hello, Baby," said Ms. Gibson. She scooped up the goose and gave it a little kiss. "Kids, come pet Baby. But be quiet. Baby doesn't like loud noises."

Everyone crowded around to pet Baby. "Ooh, she's so soft," the kids cooed. Baby snuggled in Ms. Gibson's arms, looking as sweet and gentle as her name.

Hide-and-Seek

Ms. Gibson said, "Class, while I hitch the horses to the wagon, you can play hide-and-seek in the cornstalks. Come back in ten minutes. We'll take a hayride to the pond for lunch."

"Hooray!" cheered the kids. They scattered into the corn. It was fun zigzagging around between the cornstalks.

Alf and Toc hid and jumped out to surprise Tac and Oswald.

"Fooled you!" shouted Toc as she and Alf ran off.

"Let's get back at them," said Tac.

"Yes!" said Oswald.

Oswald and Tac hid in back of some tall stalks. They did not make a sound as they waited for Alf and Toc to run by. They waited and waited and waited. At last, Oswald said, "I don't think Alf and Toc are coming."

"We'd better go back to the barnyard," said Tac. "We don't want to miss the hayride."

109

STOP! STOP! STOP!

Tac and Oswald hurried to the barnyard.

And there was Ms. Blossom, alone, waiting for them. She looked cross. "When you didn't show up, I asked Ms. Gibson to begin the hayride without you," she said. "It wasn't fair to make everyone else wait."

"We're very sorry, Ms. Blossom," said Tac and Oswald. They felt terrible. Not only had they missed the hayride, but they had made Ms. Blossom miss it too.

They could see the hay wagon going down the hill without them. "Look!" Tac said. "Maybe if we yell, they'll stop and we can catch up to them."

But everyone in the hay wagon was singing, "She'll be driving six white horses when she comes." They did not hear Tac and Oswald yelling. But Baby did, and she did <u>not</u> like it.

111

Fall on the Farm

Baby honked crossly. She flapped her powerful wings, stretched out her long neck, and ran at Tac and Oswald.

"Stop, Baby!" yelled Ms. Blossom, grabbing for the goose. But Baby stuck out her big beak and nipped at the two kids.

"Yikes!" shouted Tac. She began to run.

"Help!" shouted Oswald, running after her.

The kids ran fast, but Baby was close behind them. And Ms. Blossom was close behind Baby.

Down the hill and into the orchard they all ran. They darted between apple trees and ducked under low branches. They hopped over mushy apples on the ground. Soon Baby had chased Tac and Oswald all the way to the pond.

S-S-SLOOP! Tac skidded into the pond and fell flat on her bottom with a SPLASH! "Help!" she yowled. Then Oswald tripped and SPLASH! Down he went front first in the mucky pond. Baby seemed happy. She gave one last honk, then waddled away.

"Well," panted Ms. Blossom. "Now I see why they call this trip Fall on the Farm."

Chapter 12

All Wet

"Here comes the hay wagon," said Ms. Blossom. "Let's go meet it."

Tac and Oswald sloshed out of the pond. They slipped and slid their way up the bank. At the top, they sat on the stone wall, swinging their legs as if everything were normal. They didn't want their classmates to know they'd been chased into the pond by a goose. No one would believe that nice, gentle Baby could be so mean and scary.

"Hi," said Tac as the wagon pulled up.

"How come you're wet?" asked Toc.

"Oh, we're fine," Oswald said quickly.

"Too bad you missed the hayride," said Alf. "It was fun."

"I wish it had lasted longer," said Doc. "We got here too fast."

"We got here fast too," said Tac. "Didn't we, Oswald?"

"You can say that again!" said Oswald.

Baby Returns

A brisk breeze was blowing while the class had lunch. Oswald sat in his place shivering. He wished the breeze would dry him off, but it just made him chilly.

Tac wasn't doing much better. When she pulled out her lunch, her sandwich fell into soggy clumps. She put the mess in the trash, hoping no one saw. "Because of that goose, I'll be hungry all day!" she said to herself.

Just then, Ms. Gibson said, "Well, look who's come to visit! It's Baby!"

The kids tossed bread crusts from their sandwiches to the goose. "Here, Baby, here!" they called.

The only ones who stayed far, far away were Tac, Oswald—and Ms. Blossom!

Embarrassed

After lunch, the kids took turns mashing apples for cider.

"On the farm, we use everything," said Ms. Gibson. "For example, every bit of an apple is used. Pigs eat apple peels. Apple seeds are planted. And we use the rest of the apple in applesauce, jelly, cider, or pie."

"I could eat a whole pie myself," Tac whispered to Oswald. "My lunch was ruined."

"Mine too," said Oswald. "And I'm freezing. My pants are still wet."

"And we always share," Ms. Gibson went on. "That's the trick to living on a farm. I give my extra apples to the farmer next door. He gives me his extra pumpkins. We share food, and we share work too. On a farm, you can never be embarrassed to ask for help. You must always be willing to give it."

Tac looked at Toc's bulging backpack. She wished she weren't too embarrassed to ask Toc for the extra jacket that was inside it. But Tac was afraid that Toc would tease her. So Tac just shivered, and didn't ask.

Wild Goose Chase

When it was time to leave, Ms. Gibson gave everyone apples. Tac and Oswald were so hungry, they ate theirs before they got on the bus!

SQUISH, SQUISH went Tac's wet sneakers, and SLAP, SLAP went Oswald's wet pants as the two kids went up the steps of the bus. They flopped onto their seat.

Suddenly, they each felt a tap on the back. They turned around, expecting Alf and Toc to tease them about not being prepared for the farm trip. But Toc just handed her apple and her extra jacket to Tac, and Alf handed his apple and dry socks to Oswald.

"Thanks!" said Tac and Oswald.

"What happened to you two?" asked Alf.

"Well," said Tac. "Let's just say we went on a wild goose chase."

Good Advice

The next day, Ms. Blossom asked the children to write essays about the farm. Tac and Oswald read theirs out loud first.

Oswald said, "Our essay is called <u>Good Advice</u>."

Tac read, "Is your class going to a farm? Here are four things you should <u>not</u> do."

"One," said Oswald. "Don't tease your classmates. They're smart to be prepared."

"Two," said Tac. "Don't hide in the cornstalks to get back at someone who tricked you. You may trick yourself out of a hayride."

"Three," said Oswald. "Don't yell and make a goose so mad that it chases you into a pond, and you and your lunch get soaked."

"Four," said Tac. "Don't be too embarrassed to ask classmates for help, even if you <u>did</u> tease them. They're nice."

"In other words," Tac and Oswald said together, "Don't do what we did!"

123

Chapter 13

POW! BOOM!

Sal and Cass were kicking the soccer ball around one sunny afternoon.

POW! Sal kicked the ball to Cass. She dribbled it and then—BOOM! She blasted it into the goal.

"Good shot!" said Sal. He scooped up the ball after it bounced off the net.

"You mean <u>easy</u> shot," said Cass. "Alec would have blocked that if he were in the goal."

"Alec's a great goalie," agreed Sal. "With him on our team, I just know we'll be number one."

"Maybe," said Cass. "But we have to play the Dynamites next Saturday. They're undefeated. Ana Marco is their star, and she's fast, strong, and smart."

"We'll still win," said Sal as he bounced the ball from knee to knee. "We're good."

WHOOSH! Quick as a flash, Cass snatched the ball from Sal. "We may be good," she said, "but—" WHOMP! Cass kicked the ball and sent it flying. "Ana is <u>dynamite</u>."

Tie Score

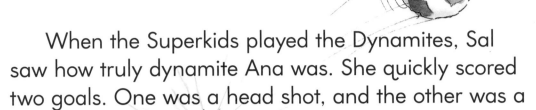

When the Superkids played the Dynamites, Sal saw how truly dynamite Ana was. She quickly scored two goals. One was a head shot, and the other was a low kick.

The Superkids did not score at all in the first half of the game, so the score was 2 to 0 at halftime.

"We've got to do better, Superkids!" Sal said as they ate their oranges.

Early in the second half, Ana nearly scored again, but Alec dove for the ball and kept it out of the goal.

Then Alec kicked the ball to Lily, and she scored.

After that, the score was stuck at 2 to 1 until the last minute of the game. Then, somehow, Icky stole the ball from Ana. He passed it to Hot Rod, who scored at the last second.

The game ended in a tie, 2 to 2.

The Superkids rushed to Hot Rod and thumped him on the back. Only Sal slumped on the bench.

"We would have won," Sal muttered, "if it weren't for that Ana."

Friend or Enemy?

"Good game!" said Ana Marco as she ran over to Cass.

Sal looked up, surprised.

"You were <u>fantastic</u>!" said Cass, hugging Ana. "Come meet my team."

Sal sat on the bench frowning as Cass introduced Ana to the other Superkids.

He frowned even more when Ana said, "Cass, can you come with my dad and me for ice cream?"

"Sure," said Cass. "I'll get my stuff and meet you at your car."

As Cass was packing up her things, Sal said, "How come you're such good buddies with Ana?"

"I know her because we're in the same Brownie troop," said Cass. "She's really nice."

"She nearly made us lose the game!" said Sal. "Don't you care?"

"Don't worry, Sal," said Cass as she turned to go. "I can be friends with Ana even if she's on the other team."

"How can you say that?" said Sal. "She's the enemy. She wrecked our game."

But Cass didn't hear him. She was running to the car. "Wait up, Ana!" she called.

Team Secrets

On Monday, Ms. Blossom led the students to the roof to water their bulbs. Sal knelt next to Ettabetta. "Hot Rod's goal was fantastic, wasn't it?" said Ettabetta.

"Yes," said Sal. "But I wish we'd won the game." He paused, and then said, "Did you know that Cass is good friends with Ana Marco?"

"You mean the star of the Dynamites?" asked Ettabetta. "She's really nice."

Sal looked worried. "Cass had better not blab any of our team secrets to her," he said. "Since we tied the last game, we have to play the Dynamites again. If Cass tells Ana any of our plays, I know they'll beat us easily."

"Cass would never do anything wrong to hurt our team," said Ettabetta.

"Not on purpose," said Sal. "But maybe by mistake."

"Oh," said Ettabetta. "Maybe we'd better tell Cass to be careful."

"And to stay away from Ana," added Sal.

Fancy Footwork

On the way home from school, Sal and Ettabetta spotted Cass and Ana talking. The two girls were looking down and kicking their feet.

"Cass has a soccer ball!" said Sal. "I bet she's showing Ana one of our secret soccer moves!" He shouted, "Cass, don't do it!"

Cass and Ana looked up. "Don't do what?" asked Cass.

"Don't show Ana any of our fancy footwork!" said Ettabetta.

Cass and Ana burst into giggles. "We're learning folk dances in Brownies," Cass explained. "I was showing Ana one of the dance steps I know."

"Oh," said Ettabetta and Sal. They felt silly.

"I'd never hurt our team by giving away secrets," said Cass. "The team's important to me."

"Cass and I can be friends," Ana added, "and still be loyal to our teams."

"Come on, Sal," said Cass as she tossed the ball to him. "Let's all just kick it around for fun."

Chapter 14

Tree Projects

Ms. Blossom's class was studying trees. They enjoyed reading about trees on the Internet and in books.

They presented what they had learned in different ways.

Trees in all Seasons

by Alec, Lily, and Hot Rod

Alec, Lily, and Hot Rod painted a mural. It showed an apple tree in all four seasons.

Alf, Doc, and Frits constructed a model of the rainforest inside a box. They used leafy twigs to look like trees.

Ettabetta, Toc, and Oswald wrote a report about women in Africa who planted more than 30 million trees.

Cass, Sal, and Tac made a chart that explained how the sun helps trees grow.

Rap Song

Icky and Tic did the coolest tree project of all. Icky wrote a play about trees, and Tic designed the costumes.

"Let's put on Icky's play!" said Hot Rod.

"Yes!" said the Superkids.

"Splendid!" said Ms. Blossom. "That will be fun!"

"Icky, please tell us there's no singing or dancing in your play," said Alf with a sigh.

Icky grinned. "There <u>is</u> one song in it," he said. "It's a rap song about paper."

"Like wrapping paper?" joked Hot Rod.

"Yes," said Icky. "It's at the very end, so it wraps up the whole show!"

"Cool!" said the kids.

We Need Trees!

A play with 3 Acts
Written by Icky
Costumes designed by Tic

Parts

Mother Nature   Johnny Appleseed

Kids   Trees   Blossoms   Snowflakes

Leaves   Apples   Apple Tree

Wadded up newspapers

Act 1: Recycle!

Four kids play with lots and lots of balled-up newspaper. Wads of paper are scattered all over the stage. Two kids dressed like trees stand in the back and watch sadly.

Kids

Kid 1: Catch it!

Kid 2: Toss it!

Kid 3: Kick it!

Kid 4: Juggle it!

All kids: Fling it all around! Throw it high!

Mother Nature runs onto the stage.

Kids

brown shirt

brown shirt

brown pants

Trees

Mother Nature

138

Mother Nature: STOP! Don't waste paper. Paper is made from trees. If you waste paper, you'll have to cut down more trees. Soon all the forests will be gone.

Trees falling down

The two trees moan and fall down. The four kids gasp and look sad. Then they pick up all the newspaper balls from the stage floor. One kid brings out a bin labeled "Recycle," and the kids put the paper balls in it.

Kid 1:   Let's pick up all this newspaper.

Kid 2:   Right! Let's recycle it.

Kid 3:   Then it can be reused.

Kid 4:   Let's save the trees!

The two trees pop up, smiling.

Mother Nature: Thank you, kids!

Mother Nature is mad!

Trees

Kids

Recycle Bin

Act 2: Gifts

Blossoms

Petal hats

Pink tutu

green tights

Mother Nature and the two trees come back onstage.

Mother Nature: Trees give us many gifts.

As Mother Nature flings tissue paper blossoms around the stage, kids dressed as blossoms come out and stand by the trees.

Mother Nature: In the spring, trees give us bright blossoms that smell nice.

Trees and Blossoms: Mmm!

As Mother Nature flings green paper leaves, the Blossoms exit and kids dressed as leaves come out and stand by the trees.

Mother Nature: In the summer, trees give us green leaves for shade.

Trees and Leaves: Ahhh!

Trees

leaf

green tights

Leaves

As Mother Nature flings paper apples around the stage, the Leaves exit and kids dressed as apples come out and stand by the trees.

Mother Nature: In the fall, trees give us apples to eat.

Trees and Apples: Yum! Yum!

As Mother Nature flings cotton balls around the stage, the Apples exit and kids dressed as snowflakes come out and stand by the trees.

Mother Nature: In the winter, trees get snow on them. We use it for . . . SNOWBALLS!

The Blossoms, Leaves, and Apples return to the stage to have a wild snowball fight with Mother Nature, the Trees, and the Snowflakes using the cotton balls.

Apples

← stem hat

red sweatpants (stuffed with pillows)

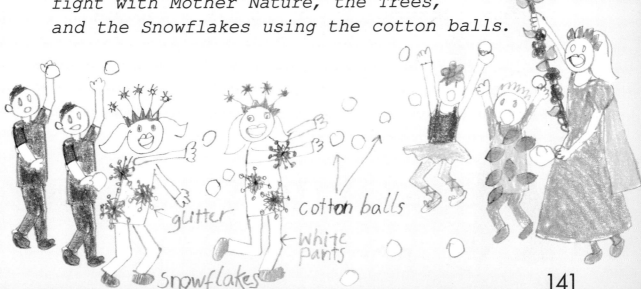

glitter

cotton balls

← white pants

snowflakes

Act 3: Johnny Appleseed

Johnny Appleseed and a kid dressed as an apple tree enter. Johnny waves.

Apple Tree: Hi, there! This is Johnny Appleseed. Long ago, he walked all over the country planting apple seeds.

Johnny kneels down and pretends to plant seeds.

Apple Tree: That's why he's called...

Johnny: Johnny Appleseed! I love trees. It makes me sad to see how people waste trees today. I want kids to respect trees and not hurt them. Don't waste paper because paper comes from trees.

Apple Tree: Trees like me!

Johnny: Right! Just think of all the kinds of paper we waste: newspaper, notebook paper, writing paper...

Tree

hat →

sack of apple seeds

shirt
← overalls

Johnny Appleseed

← hiking boots

142

Apple Tree: Wrapping paper!

Johnny: This tree and I thought of a rap song to wrap up the play and to remind you not to waste paper.

Apple Tree and Johnny make rapper moves as they chant.

Apple Tree: Don't waste paper!

Johnny: Paper comes from trees!

Apple Tree: Don't waste paper!

Johnny: Trees are what we need!

Apple Tree: Don't waste paper!

Johnny: Recycle it, please!

Apple Tree: *(gestures to audience to join in loudly)* Recycle it!

Johnny: Reuse it!

Johnny and Apple Tree: Respect all trees!

Respect all Trees!

Johnny →

Respect all trees

← Tree

Chapter 15

The Star

"We must decide who will be Mother Nature and Johnny Appleseed," Ms. Blossom told the class.

All the girls shot their hands into the air and called out, "I want to be Mother Nature!"

But then Cass said, "Tic designed the costumes. So she should be Mother Nature."

The other girls didn't mind too much. They knew Cass was right.

"Well, I want to be Johnny Appleseed most," said Hot Rod. "He's the star of the play."

Hot Rod pretended to plant seeds in the floor, in the air, and even in Sal's hair! Most of the kids laughed. Hot Rod was so clever and funny.

"Let's take a vote," said Ms. Blossom. "All for Hot Rod being Johnny Appleseed say yes!"

"YES!" shouted all the Superkids, except two.

Hot Rod shouted, "Hooray!"

And Icky didn't shout anything at all.

145

It Isn't Fair!

"It isn't fair!" Icky said to himself as he trudged home. "I wanted to be Johnny Appleseed. I wrote the play, and I wanted to be the star. But Hot Rod grabbed that part, so now I'm just the apple tree."

Icky felt madder and madder as he went along. He remembered the soccer game against the Dynamites when he had stolen the ball and passed it to Hot Rod so Hot Rod could score in the last seconds of the game. Everyone had run up to Hot Rod and praised him for scoring the goal, which he never could have done without Icky's pass. But no one had praised Icky for anything.

"Hot Rod was the big hero of the game, and now he's going to be the star of my play," Icky muttered. "He's a big show-off!"

Hot Rod Messes Up

The first day of play practice went OK. Icky had to admit that Hot Rod was good as Johnny Appleseed. But two days later, Ms. Blossom said that the kids could not read from their scripts anymore. They had to memorize their lines. What a disaster! Hot Rod could <u>not</u> remember what he was supposed to say.

"Boys, I want to hear you do your rap song," Ms. Blossom said to Icky and Hot Rod. "Icky, you begin."

"OK," said Icky. "Don't waste paper!"

Hot Rod looked confused. "Uh . . . Trees are what we need?" he said at last.

"No!" snapped Icky. "You're supposed to say, 'Paper comes from trees.'"

"Oh, right," said Hot Rod. "Sorry I messed up. I'll remember it next time."

But he never did.

So one afternoon, Icky went to Ms. Blossom. "Hot Rod keeps wrecking our act," Icky said crossly. "He forgets most of his lines, so I can't do mine right."

"Getting mad isn't going to do any good," said Ms. Blossom kindly. "You and Hot Rod will have to find a way to make your act work. You two have to be a team."

On the Ball

Icky and Hot Rod were kicking the ball around after soccer practice. Icky was still annoyed at Hot Rod, so it felt good to kick the ball to him really hard. WHOMP!

"Whoa!" said Hot Rod. "That was a wild kick."

"Sorry," said Icky.

"No problem," said Hot Rod. He hesitated, and then said, "I'm sorry too. I know I keep forgetting my lines in the play. I wish I could remember them as well as I remember soccer moves."

And that gave Icky a good idea. Suddenly, he was not annoyed anymore. He remembered how Ms. Blossom told him he and Hot Rod had to work as a team in the play. "I've got it," said Icky. "Let's practice our lines and our soccer moves at the same time."

"How can we do that?" asked Hot Rod.

"I'll say my line and kick the ball to you," said Icky. "Without letting the ball stop, you kick it back to me and say <u>your</u> line."

"OK," said Hot Rod.

The boys had to think fast and move fast to keep the rhythm going. "This is hard," panted Hot Rod.

"Yes," joked Icky, "but it keeps us on the ball."

Don't waste paper!

Paper comes from trees!

Don't waste paper!

Trees are what we need!

The Switch-Kick Trick

Hot Rod and Icky practiced whenever they had a chance. At first, Icky would say Hot Rod's lines along with him. But soon Hot Rod was remembering his lines just fine.

"Thanks, Icky," he said. "Kicking the ball while we said our lines was a good trick. Now <u>I'll</u> teach <u>you</u> a cool soccer trick. It's called the switch kick."

"OK," said Icky.

"You run next to me," said Hot Rod. "I'll pretend to pass the ball <u>away</u> from you. Then I'll switch and use the outside of my foot to pass it <u>to</u> you, like this." POOM! Hot Rod did a switch kick and shot the ball to Icky.

"Smooth move!" said Icky.

"We've got to be a team on this," said Hot Rod, "or it won't work."

"Let's try it again," said Icky. "I want to practice our tricky switch kick."

Chapter 16

The Day of the Play

At last the day came when the Superkids were going to present Icky's play. The auditorium was packed. There was lots of action backstage, behind the curtain. Everyone was buzzing with excitement.

The kids who were Snowflakes jiggled to make their glitter sparkle. The Blossoms hopped to flutter their petals. The Apples bounced off each other's padded tummies.

Tic was a perfect Mother Nature in her green robe and her crown of leaves. The funniest costume was Hot Rod's. As Johnny Appleseed, he wore overalls, boots, and best of all, a cooking pot as a hat!

Hot Rod grinned at Icky. "Knock, knock," said Hot Rod as he banged his fist on the pot on his head.

"Who's there?" asked Icky.

"Anita," said Hot Rod.

"Anita, who?" asked Icky.

"Anita tree," said Hot Rod, making a goofy face. "And you look like a good one!"

On with the Show!

The heavy curtain went up.

"Ooh," said the kids in the audience when they saw Mother Nature and the Trees.

Act One went well. Tic spoke her lines as Mother Nature in a loud, clear voice. In Act Two, the Superkids who were Blossoms, Leaves, Apples, and Snowflakes changed positions smoothly. The audience loved the snowball fight.

Soon, the time had come for Act Three, the act with Icky as a talking apple tree and Hot Rod as Johnny Appleseed.

"I hope Hot Rod remembers his lines," Icky thought as Hot Rod walked proudly out onto the stage.

"Icky," someone whispered. "You're supposed to be out there too! Go!" Hands shoved Icky from the back. Before he knew it, he was in front of the audience.

Then the strangest thing happened.

Sidekick, Sidestick

Icky couldn't walk. He couldn't talk. He couldn't catch his breath. He was frozen with stage fright.

Hot Rod waited for Icky to say his line. Icky said nothing. Hot Rod nudged him. Still Icky said nothing.

So Hot Rod began to talk. "Hi, there!" he said. "I'm Johnny Appleseed, and this is my sidekick, or rather my side<u>stick</u>. He's quiet. Well, who's ever heard of a noisy tree?"

The audience laughed.

Hot Rod kept talking, saying what Icky was meant to say. "Long ago, I walked all over the country planting apple seeds."

Hot Rod paused. He pretended to plant seeds, just as he was supposed to. He hoped that Icky would be ready to say his next line. But Icky wasn't ready. So Hot Rod went on. "That's why I'm called Johnny Appleseed. I love trees. Trees like this one." He thumped Icky on the back. "Right, buddy?"

Icky could only nod miserably.

159

Hot Rod Saves the Play

Hot Rod had to think fast. He and Icky were supposed to do the rap song next. It was clear that Icky was still scared stiff, and Hot Rod couldn't do the song by himself. So Hot Rod took a chance.

"My friends and I have made up a rap song for you," he said to the audience. "They're all going to come out here onstage now and help me perform it."

A voice from offstage whispered, "What?"

"I said," boomed Hot Rod, "everyone will come out here and help me. NOW!"

There was lots of scuffling. Then Mother Nature, the Blossoms, the Apples, the Trees, the Leaves, and the Snowflakes hurried onstage.

Hot Rod began, "Don't waste paper!"

"Paper comes from trees!" chanted the kids. They sounded a little unsure. But by the time they got to the last line, they were good and loud. The Apples even started to do rap moves.

At the end, the audience clapped and cheered.
Icky turned to Hot Rod and whispered,

Thanks, Hot Rod!
You saved the play!

Teamwork

The next Saturday, the Superkids played the Dynamites again. The Superkids got off to a good start. Sal scored on a high shot to the corner of the goal. But then the Dynamites exploded into action! Alec blocked three tough shots from Ana, but then she slammed one by him, making the score 1 to 1.

"Oh, no! Not another tie," moaned Sal at halftime.

It was the same in the second half. No matter how hard they tried, the Superkids couldn't score. Then, with just a few seconds left, Icky passed the ball to Hot Rod, who dribbled quickly down the field. It looked as if Hot Rod was going to go for the goal. Then—POOM! He did the switch-kick trick and passed the ball to Icky, who scored!

The Superkids won the game!

"Hooray for Icky," they cheered. "We're number one! Go Superkids!"

Ana rushed up to Icky and Hot Rod. "Awesome trick," she said. "How did you two get so good at that play?"

The boys looked at each other, laughed, and said, "Teamwork!"